The Big Bible Sticker Book

by Jan Godfrey
and Paula Doherty

CONCORDIA PUBLISHING HOUSE · SAINT LOUIS

A Wonderful World

Genesis 1–2

What a wonderful world our great God made long, long ago!

"Let there be light," God said. And there was light!

"Let there be rivers, mountains, and seas; leaves, flowers, and trees," said God. And there were all those things!

Then, God made the sun, moon, and stars. He made day and night.

He made wet, slippery fishes, colorful birds, and dainty butterflies. God made animals with swishy tails or tickly whiskers. Some made growly noises, and some made no sound at all.

Last of all, God made people to love Him and to look after His wonderful world.

"The world I've made is very, very good," said God.

And then God rested.

One of the animals is in the wrong place. Put the monkey sticker on top of it to hide the mistake.

Complete the picture by adding the other animal stickers and the sun sticker.

Noah's Ark

Genesis 6–9

It's going to rain," God said to Noah. "The people I made have been bad and unkind. But I promise I will keep you safe. Build an ark for your family and all the animals."

Noah loved God and believed Him. So Noah built the ark. His family and all the animals went into the ark, two by two by two by two.

Then it rained, just as God said it would. It rained and rained and rained for forty days and nights! The whole world filled with water. But Noah's ark floated safely.

At last, it stopped raining, and the ark rested on dry land. God sent a wonderful shining rainbow and said He would never flood the world that way again.

God always keeps His promises.

Find six
stickers
to pair up
all the missing
animals.

Abraham's Long Journey

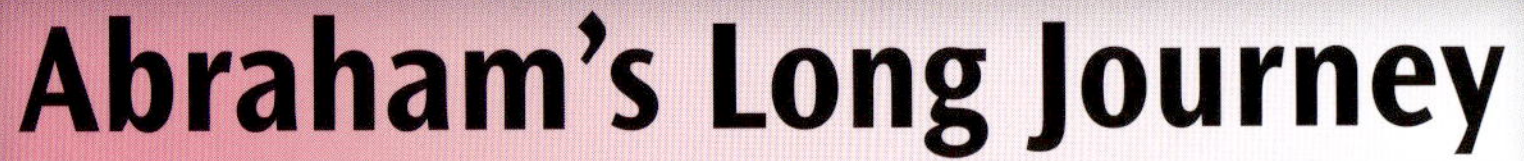

Genesis 12, 15, 18, 21

A long time after Noah, God spoke to a man named Abraham. "Take your wife, Sarah, and go far away to the land of Canaan. I will take care of you, and I will bless you."

So Abraham went to Canaan.

"Look at all those zillions of stars!" said God. "One day you will have a son, and from him will follow zillions more families, as many as the stars. I promise."

One day, three messengers from God appeared. "This time next year, you will have a baby," they said.

"I'm far too old!" laughed Sarah.

The next year, Sarah laughed again, but this time because she was so happy. She and Abraham had a baby, just as God had promised. They named him Isaac.

Use the stickers to make a tent like the one in the big picture.

Place the star sticker in the sky.

Find room in the big picture
for these four animals.

Esau and Jacob

Genesis 25, 27

Issac and his wife, Rebekah, had twin sons named Esau and Jacob. Esau liked hunting wild animals. Jacob liked cooking them.

Because Esau was born first, he would lead the family one day. But Jacob wanted to be the leader too.

Isaac was very old, and he couldn't see very well. Jacob played a trick on him. He dressed up as Esau and brought Isaac a bowl of delicious stew.

"Here you are, Father," Jacob said.

"Is that you, Esau?" said old Isaac.

"Yes," fibbed Jacob. "Don't I feel like Esau? Don't I smell like Esau?"

"God bless you, my son. You will lead my family when I am gone," said Isaac.

Jacob had tricked Isaac into giving him what was Esau's. When Esau found out, he was very angry. When Isaac found out that Jacob had lied, he was very sad.

Jacob had to leave home. But although Jacob had done something bad, God protected him.

Put the fire under the cooking pot.

Put two goats just outside the tent.

Put Esau with his spear on the path under the trees.

Put the jar on the box table.

Put the pot on the floor of the tent.

Put the fruit in the bowl.

Jacob's Favorite Son

Genesis 37

After a time, Jacob returned home, and Esau forgave him. Then Jacob had a big family of his own—twelve sons and a daughter! Jacob liked his son Joseph best of all.

One day, Jacob gave Joseph a special coat. Joseph's brothers were jealous of him, and they did not like that their father had given Joseph something special.

Then Joseph had dreams where all his brothers bowed down to him. Joseph told his brothers about his dreams. His brothers didn't like that very much either.

"Who does Joseph think he is?" they complained. "He thinks he's so important."

The brothers made a plan. They waited for the right moment, and then they grabbed Joseph and threw him down into a pit. Then they told their father that Joseph was dead.

Jacob was very, very sad.

But God was with Joseph and took care of him.

Complete the picture below by adding sheep to the hill.

Add stickers to the bottom picture to show what happened to Joseph.

God Takes Care of Joseph

Genesis 39, 41–45

Joseph's brothers sold him to be a slave in Egypt, a land that was far, far away. Things went very badly for Joseph for a while. But God did not forget him.

One night, the king of Egypt dreamed strange dreams about corn and cows. Joseph helped him understand what his dreams meant.

Joseph said, "Your dreams mean that one day the corn will stop growing. We must save lots of corn before then so we won't be hungry later."

The king was pleased with Joseph and made him a very important man.

Later, after the corn stopped growing, Joseph's brothers came to Egypt to buy corn. Many years had passed, so they didn't recognize their little brother. But Joseph recognized them and told them who he was.

"I know you wanted to hurt me," he told them. "But God was taking care of us all the time. Let us be a family again. Now we can all live in Egypt where there is plenty to eat."

Put the red cushion on the throne.

Give the servant a fan to hold.

Complete the picture by adding the old man's missing feet.

Add the correct stickers.
Jacob
Joseph

The Princess and the Baby

Exodus 1–2

Waahhh!!!" cried little baby Moses.

"Ssshh," said his mother anxiously. "The cruel king and his soldiers might hear you. He doesn't like baby boys. He is afraid they might grow big and fight him!"

"Waahhh!" cried baby Moses again.

His mother made a waterproof basket for Moses and hid him beside the river. "God will take care of him," she told Moses' big sister, Miriam.

After a time, the king's daughter came to the river. Miriam was hiding in the weeds so she could see what happened to Moses.

"Oh! A baby!" said the princess. "I will take him home to live in the palace."

"You'll need a nurse to help take care of him," said Miriam. She ran and fetched her mother—baby Moses' own mother—to be the nurse.

God had kept baby Moses safe.

Find four frog stickers to add to the river.

Put the baby Moses in the basket.

Add the papyrus to the River Nile.

Plagues in Egypt

Exodus 3, 6–12

Moses grew up to be a wise leader who loved God. But God's people were still slaves in Egypt.

One day, God spoke to Moses from a holy burning bush. "Tell the cruel king to let My people go free," said God.

Moses did as God said. He went to the king and asked and asked, but the king kept saying NO!

Then some horrible things happened. People couldn't drink from the river. All the fish died. Frogs and flies were everywhere—even inside people's houses! Clouds of insects ate all the crops. People became ill, and animals became ill too.

Huge hailstones fell from the sky, and the sun hid and everyone sat in the dark for days. Eventually people died.

"Now will you let my people go?" Moses asked the king.

"Oh," said the king. "Just take your people and GO AWAY!"

At last, Moses led God's people safely out of Egypt.

Use the stickers to create a plague of flies and frogs.

Crossing the Big, Wide Sea

Exodus 14–20

Moses led the people, and God led Moses. They walked and walked, and at last they all reached the Red Sea.

"It's deep and wide. How will we get across it?" everyone asked.

But God made it possible for them to cross the water. Moses lifted a special wooden stick, and the wind blew the waves back so all the people could cross safely on the path through the sea.

God kept taking care of His people. He sent special food called manna for them to eat. And there was fresh water from a rock to drink.

One day, Moses climbed a mountain. At the top of the mountain, he talked with God. God gave Moses ten important rules—the Commandments—to teach people how to live with God and with one another.

1

2

3

4

Place the right face sticker in each circle.

Add more fish stickers to the waves.

4
3
2
1

The Boy Who Listened

1 Samuel 1–3

Hannah loved her son, Samuel, very much. She knew that God had special plans for him.

When Samuel was old enough, Hannah took him to the temple where the old priest, Eli, would teach him and look after him.

One night, Samuel woke up. "Samuel!" called a voice. He thought it was Eli.

"I didn't call for you," said Eli.

Then Samuel heard the voice again. He went back to Eli.

"But I didn't call you," said Eli.

Then Samuel heard the voice call his name again, so he went one more time to Eli. This time, Eli knew it was God who had spoken to Samuel. He told Samuel to go back and listen to what God had to say.

Samuel always listened to God after that. Hannah was right. God did have special plans for him.

Find these stickers to set the table below.

Add this little mouse to the picture.

Find the sticker to match the shape.
What kind of animal is this?

The Youngest Son

1 Samuel 8, 16

Samuel grew up to be a great prophet who led God's people.

"You must choose the next king," said God to Samuel, "one who is truly good and wise inside his heart."

Seven of Jesse's sons stood in front of Samuel. They were all tall and strong. It was hard to choose the best one!

"Is it this one?" Samuel prayed. "Or that one?"

"No, not this one," said God. "Nor that one."

Not one of those seven sons was to be king.

"Do you have more sons?" Samuel asked Jesse.

David, the youngest son, came in from the fields.

"David is good and wise inside his heart," said God. "Choose him."

Samuel sprinkled David with olive oil as a special sign that he would one day be king. God was always with David.

Complete the small picture by adding the six other sons. Use the big picture to guide you.

David and the Giant

1 Samuel 17

Goliath was fierce and ugly and bad and a giant of a man! Everyone was frightened of Goliath.

As King Saul's soldiers watched Goliath coming closer, they shivered and quivered and quaked!

"I'll fight him," said David bravely. "God has helped me fight lions and bears. He'll help me now."

"You? Fight me?!" roared Goliath. "You're only a boy! And you're not even wearing proper armor!"

"But I come in God's name," said David. He took five stones from a stream and whirled them around in a sling.

Wham! Goliath toppled to the ground, and all his soldiers ran away. God had helped David defeat the giant.

Find stickers to represent the two armies.

Find the stickers of David and Goliath to complete the picture.

Use the stickers to finish dressing the giant.

Elijah and the Ravens

1 Kings 17–18

You say you don't believe in the God who made all the earth?" said Elijah to bad King Ahab. "Now it won't rain for a long, long time. Not until God says so. The crops won't grow, and you will be hungry. You wait and see."

It stopped raining—just as God had said—so God told Elijah to go and hide by a little stream.

"You'll have drinking water there," said God. "And ravens will bring you food."

Elijah drank fresh water from the little stream. And every morning and every evening, friendly ravens brought him food, just as God had said.

God took care of Elijah until King Ahab believed in God again, and the rain fell once more upon the earth.

Find stickers to surround Elijah with ravens.

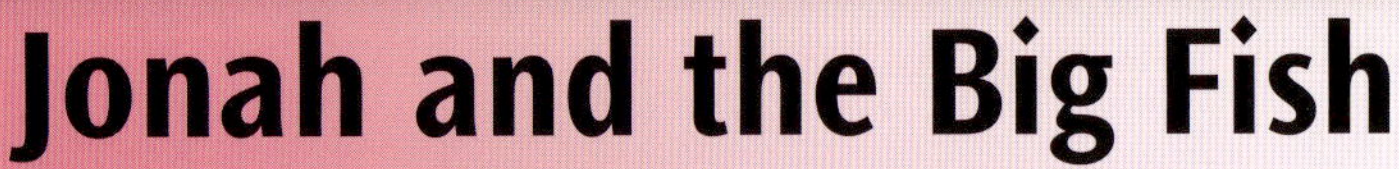

Jonah and the Big Fish

Jonah 1–4

God told Jonah to take a message to the people in Nineveh, where people did bad, wrong things. But Jonah didn't want to go there! He sailed to Joppa instead.

A huge storm came. Jonah knew why.

"The storm came because I disobeyed God," Jonah told the sailors. "Throw me into the sea!" They did, and the storm stopped.

But God took care of Jonah. He sent a very large fish to swallow him. Jonah stayed inside the fish for three days. It was very dark, but Jonah knew God had saved him.

"I'm sorry," Jonah said to God. "I should have gone to Nineveh. Please forgive me, Lord."

Then—woossssh!—the big fish spat Jonah onto dry land.

Jonah went to Nineveh, and the people there listened to him about God. They were sorry, too, and changed how they were behaving. God forgave them.

Complete the picture by adding the fish stickers.
Complete the picture by adding the Jonah sticker.

Daniel and the Lions

Daniel 6

Far away in Babylon, Daniel worked for the king. The king's men didn't like Daniel. They knew that Daniel loved and worshiped God.

"We worship you, oh king!" they said. "But Daniel does not worship you. Send him to the lions because he worships God instead." So Daniel was thrown into the lions' den.

The king didn't sleep well that night. He thought about Daniel and the hungry lions. Early the next morning, he went to the lions' den.

"Daniel, are you there?" the king asked.

"Here I am, king," said Daniel. "God sent His angels to protect me from the lions."

The king couldn't believe his eyes. But it was true. The lions hadn't touched Daniel. "Your God really is the true and living God!" said the king. "Everyone in my kingdom will worship Him from now on!"

Find these two stickers to show the difference between a female lion and a male lion.

Male lion

Female lion

Fill the lions' den with these
three lion stickers
and a mouse.

An Angel Visits Mary

Luke 1

One ordinary day, a girl named Mary had a very big surprise. God's angel Gabriel came to visit her. Mary was really afraid.

"Do not fear," Gabriel said. "I have a message for you from God. You are going to have a baby—the Son of God Himself! He will be called Jesus."

This was a big surprise! And Mary was very happy that God had chosen her to be the mother of His Son. She said to the angel, "Let it be done according to what God says."

She ran to tell her cousin Elizabeth, and they praised God together.

"You're a great and wonderful God," sang Mary. "You have done wonderful things for me. I praise You!"

Put the cat sticker on the window ledge.

Put the hen and her chicks near the food.

Find room in the picture to add this large sheep and chicken.

No Room at the Inn

Luke 2

One dark night in a stable in Bethlehem, Mary's baby was born. She called Him Jesus, just as the angel had said.

Angels appeared in the sky where some shepherds were watching their sheep. "God's Son is born in Bethlehem!" the angels sang.

The shepherds in the fields ran to find Him. They went to the stable and looked in the manger.

There was God's Son, the newborn baby Jesus, lying in the hay and wrapped in cloths.

The shepherds knelt and worshiped Him.

"God's angels sang to us," they told Mary and Joseph. "They told us where to find you."

Mary smiled as they told their story.

Then the shepherds went back to their fields, praising God and telling everyone they saw about Jesus.

Put this shepherd boy near the baby Jesus.

Add the baby Jesus to the manger.

Add the chicken to the roof of the stable.

Add the star stickers to the sky.

What was the camel carrying?
Find the right sticker.

Special Visitors

Matthew 2

Far, far away, some wise and clever men saw a special star high in the sky. "This is a sign from God," they said.

"It means a new King has been born," they said.

"We will go worship Him and take gifts," they said.

The Wise Men took their camels and their gifts, and they followed the big, bright star that was high in the sky. At last, the star led them to Mary and Joseph and the baby Jesus.

The Wise Men knelt down and worshiped the baby King. They gave Him presents: gold and frankincense and myrrh. These were special gifts for a very special baby, God's Son.

Add the star sticker that led the Wise Men into the night sky.

Add the goat sticker to the picture above.

Add these three visitors to the picture above.

Jesus Chooses Friends

Matthew 4; Luke 5

Jesus grew up and began teaching people about God and His kingdom.

One day, Jesus went to the seashore. Some fishermen were there washing their nets.

"Take your boat out further and put your nets in deeper water," Jesus said.

"We've been fishing all night and haven't caught anything," said Peter. "But we will do as You say."

So they tried again and caught so many fish that their nets nearly broke! The fishermen couldn't believe their eyes.

"Come with Me," Jesus said, "and I will teach you how to be fishers of men. We will tell people all about God and His love for us."

And that's exactly what they did.

Complete the picture by adding these stickers.

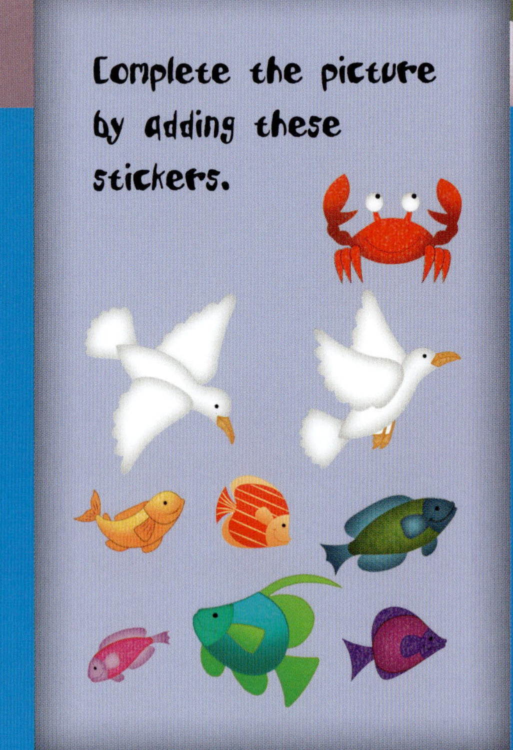

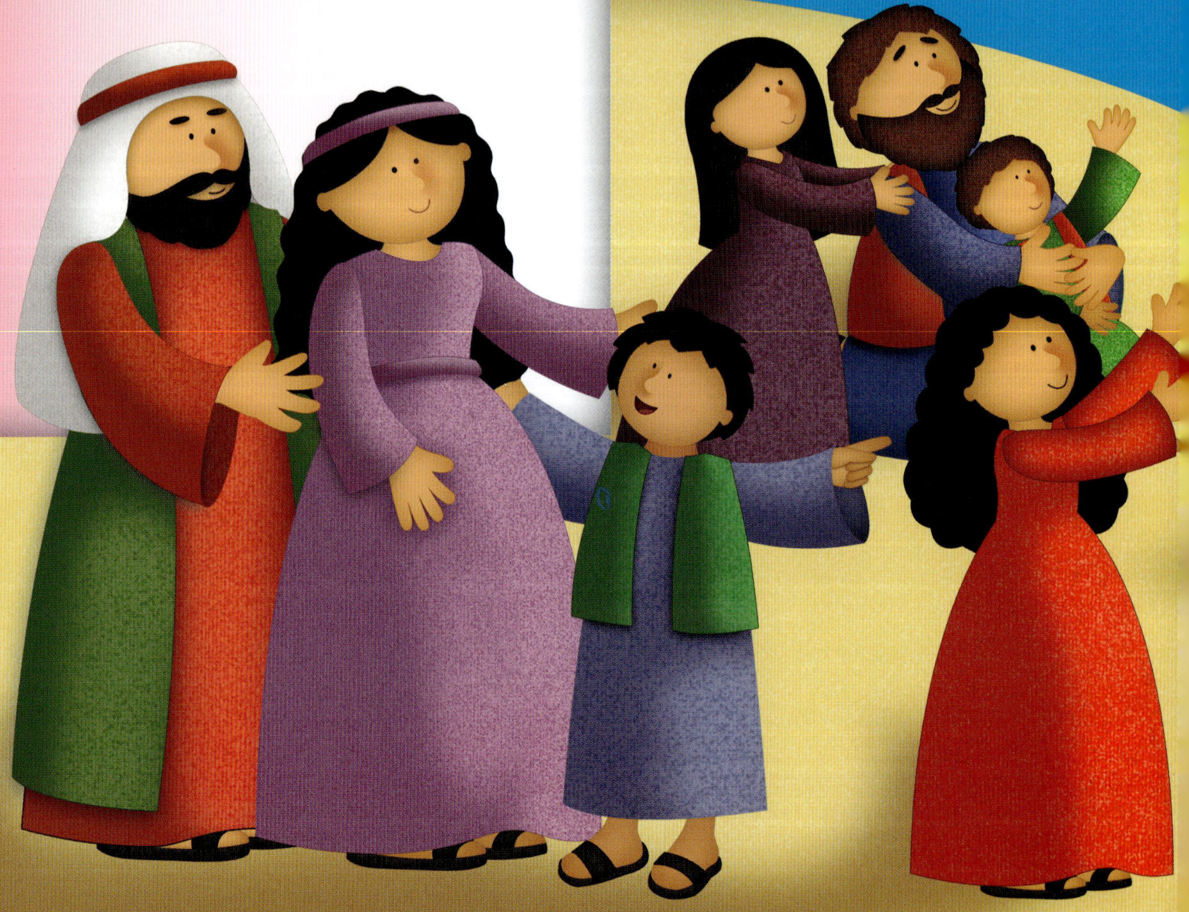

God Loves You

Matthew 6

Jesus went throughout the land to teach people about God and His kingdom. Many people came to hear Jesus talk.

One day, Jesus sat on a mountain and talked about how much God loves His people.

"Look at the birds in the sky," Jesus said. "God makes sure they always have food. God always takes care of them.

"You are more important to God than the birds. God will always take care of you too. You can ask Him for the things you need. God knows what you need."

Jesus taught the people to put God first.

Complete the picture by adding butterflies and flowers.

Add the red sash to Jesus' robe.

Put the sun in the sky.

The Hole in the Roof

Mark 2

Five friends wanted to see Jesus. One friend couldn't walk. The others carried him on a mattress. They found Jesus in a house where He was talking to people.

"The house is too crowded!" said one.

"We'll never get near Jesus!" said another.

"What will we do?" one friend asked.

The fourth friend said, "Let's make a hole in the roof!"

They scrabbled and scraped, and then they used ropes to lower their friend down to Jesus.

Jesus spoke to the man. "God forgives everything you've done wrong. Now pick up your mat and go home."

And to everyone's surprise, the man picked up his mat and went home! Jesus had forgiven the man's sins and healed the man so he could walk.

Add a lamp to the shelf.

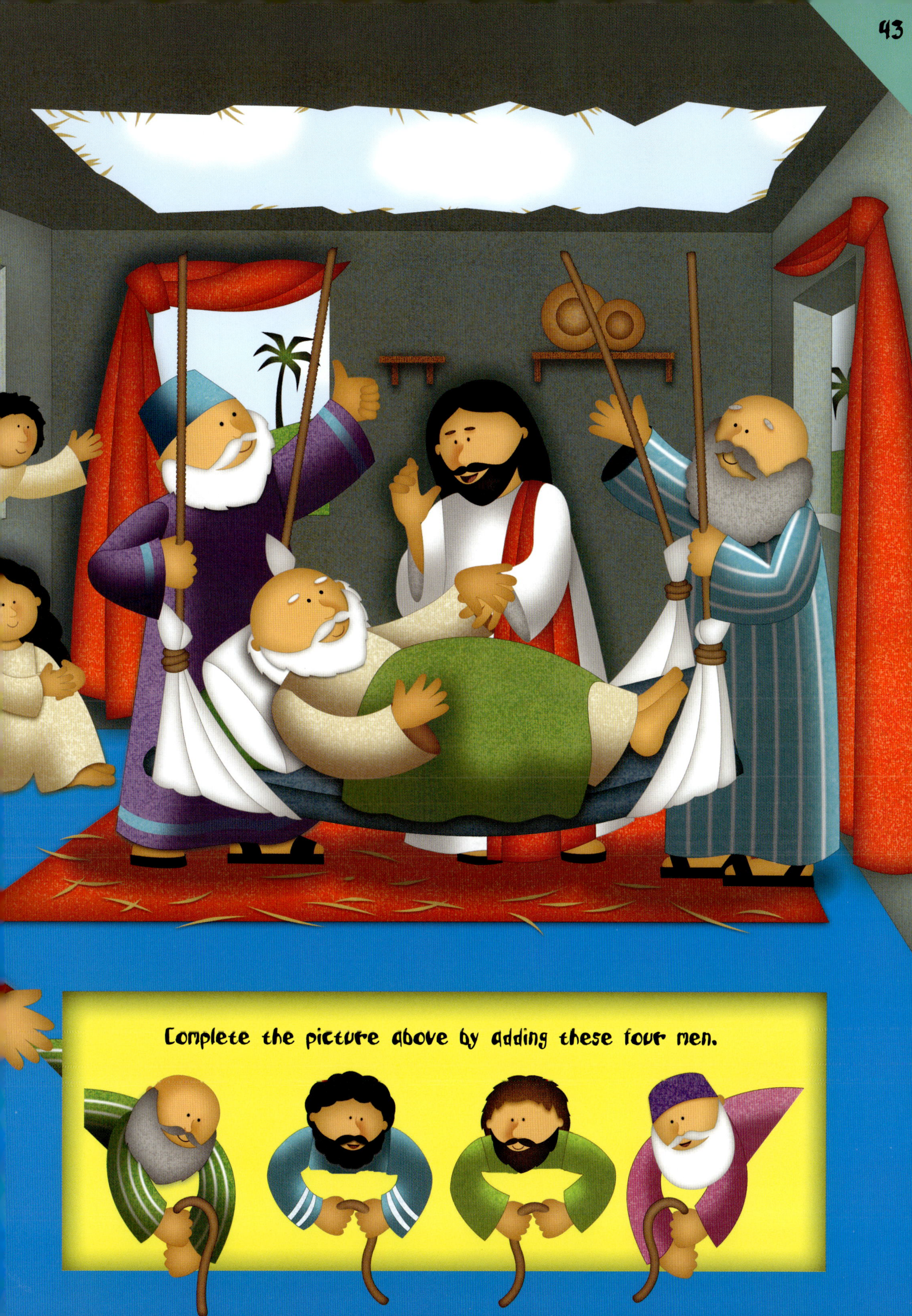
Complete the picture above by adding these four men.

The Very Scary Storm

Mark 4

One calm, quiet evening, Jesus and His friends sailed across a big lake. It had been such a busy day that Jesus soon fell asleep in the boat.

Then the wind blew harder and little splashy waves grew higher and higher. The little boat was tossed up and down, up and down. Suddenly it was a very scary storm! Jesus' friends were terrified.

"Wake up, Lord! Help us! We're going to drown!" they shouted.

Jesus woke up and stood in the boat. "Be quiet!" He said to the wind and waves. Immediately the storm died down, and the lake was calm and peaceful again.

Jesus' friends were amazed. "Even the weather does what Jesus tells it to do!" they said.

These two men are missing from the boat. Find the stickers to put them back where they belong.

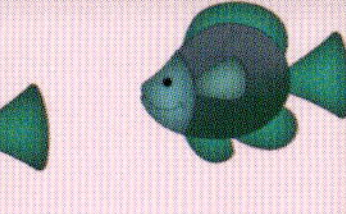

Add fish stickers like this to the ocean.

Find a sticker shaped like this to discover what's flying in the air at the back of the boat.

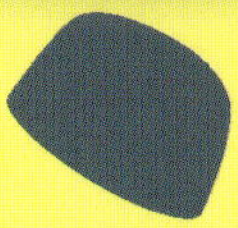

Jairus's Little Girl

Mark 5

One day, a man named Jairus came running to Jesus.

"Please come quickly!" said Jairus. "My little daughter is very, very ill!"

They set off to Jairus's house, but people crowded around Jesus and interrupted at every step. Jairus grew more and more impatient. His daughter might die!

When they finally got to the house, they heard people crying. They were too late!

"Shhh," said Jesus as He went into the house. "She's only asleep. Come on, little girl, get up."

And she did! Jesus took her hand and helped her to her feet.

"She'll be hungry," said Jesus. "She needs something to eat."

Jesus had healed her. Her parents were very, very happy, and they thanked God.

Find a sticker that fits in the window.

Find the sticker that fits on the shelf. What is it?

Add the three missing items to the carpet.

The Very Big Picnic

John 6

Many people had come to hear Jesus. The crowd grew bigger and bigger until there were thousands of people. Everyone wanted to hear Jesus teach about God.

The people listened all day. Jesus taught them many things.

Now they were hungry, but they hadn't brought any food with them, and there was nowhere to buy any.

Then a little boy offered to share his picnic. "Please take this," he said to Jesus. The boy held up five bread rolls and two small fish.

Add the sticker of the boy who offered Jesus his lunch.

"Thank you," said Jesus. "And thank You, God."

Jesus had His friends give out the food to all the people. There was enough food for everyone!

Jesus had turned the boy's small meal into enough food to feed all the people who were there. There was even food left over.

It was a wonderful miracle!

The Man in the Tree

Luke 19

Nobody liked Zacchaeus very much. He was a rich tax collector, and he cheated people out of money.

Today Jesus was coming! Zacchaeus wanted to see Him. But Zacchaeus was short, and he couldn't see over the crowd. So he climbed into a tree.

Just as Zacchaeus looked down through the branches, Jesus stopped and looked up!

"Come down, Zacchaeus," said Jesus. "I'm going to your house. We will have dinner together."

Zacchaeus happily scrambled down from the tree and took Jesus to his house for dinner.

Zacchaeus promised that he would never cheat again. "I'll give some money to poor people too," said Zacchaeus.

Everyone was surprised that Jesus went with Zacchaeus, but Jesus said, "I've come to save people like Zacchaeus."

Put the butterfly stickers in the sky.

Find the squirrel stickers and put them in the tree.

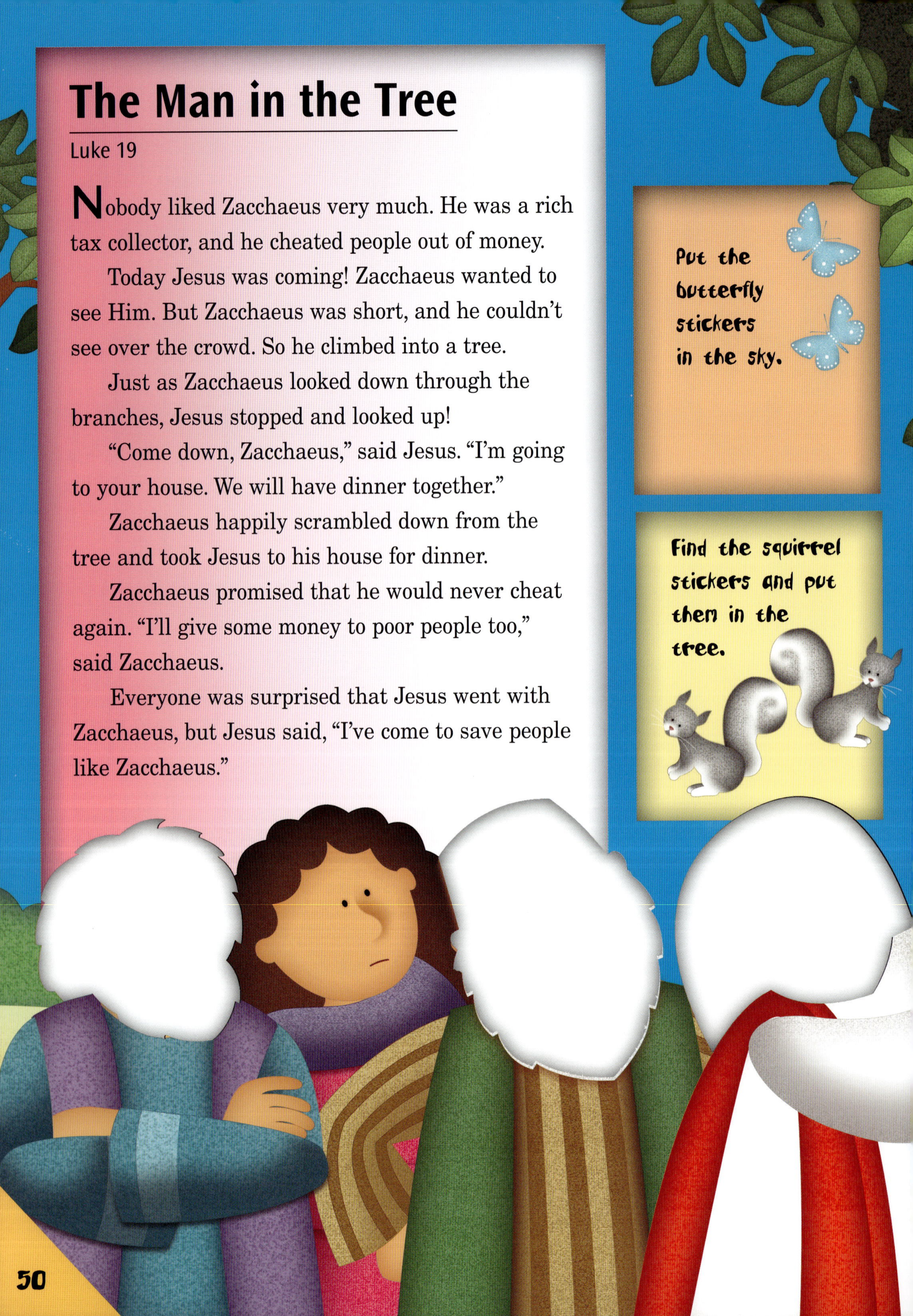

Match the head stickers
to the people opposite.

Riding on a Donkey

Matthew 21

Find stickers of people to put in the windows below.

Jesus was riding on a donkey. He and His friends were going to Jerusalem.

Crowds of people stood by the road—men and women and children, happy and excited people, shouting and cheering. Jesus was coming!

"Hosanna!" they shouted. "Hosanna to Lord Jesus!"

The crowd grew bigger and bigger, noisier and noisier. People threw down their coats in front of Jesus and waved palm branches. They pushed and crowded to see the parade for Jesus.

They shouted and cheered. "Praise King Jesus!"

But some people were not happy. They were not Jesus' friends. They started to plan to get rid of Jesus.

Find palm stickers like these and place them in the hands of the people in the crowd.

Add bird stickers to the sky.

The Last Supper

Mark 14:12–25

Jesus and His friends shared a special meal. They ate lamb and herbs and bread and had red wine to drink. "Remember Me every time you eat bread and drink wine together," said Jesus to them. "This is My body and My blood, given for you for the forgiveness of sins."

Jesus knew that one of His friends was planning something very, very bad. "Soon one of you will give Me away to My enemies," He said.

His disciples shook their heads. "I would never do such a thing!" said Peter. "None of us would!"

But Jesus knew that Judas would betray Him.

Can you find space on the big shelf for these two plates?

Put the food and
drink on the table.

Add the
oil lamps
to the shelf.

Praying in the Garden

Mark 14:32–50

After supper, Jesus' friends walked with Him in a garden nearby.

Jesus was sad, so He prayed.

"Please help Me, Father God," said Jesus. "I know that what I have to do will be very hard to do. But I will do whatever You want of Me."

Meanwhile, Jesus' friends fell asleep, one by one. "Couldn't you stay awake to pray with Me for a little while?" asked Jesus sadly.

But, suddenly, His friends woke up! There were noisy, angry voices. There were clattering swords and spears and bright lanterns coming into the garden.

And there was Judas, who had once been Jesus' friend. Judas brought the soldiers to take Jesus away.

Complete the picture below by adding these stickers.

Complete the picture below by adding these stickers.

Add the sticker of Judas leading the band of armed men.

Place the stickers in the empty boxes next to the caption that describes it.
There are seven of these in the picture.
There are four of these in the picture.

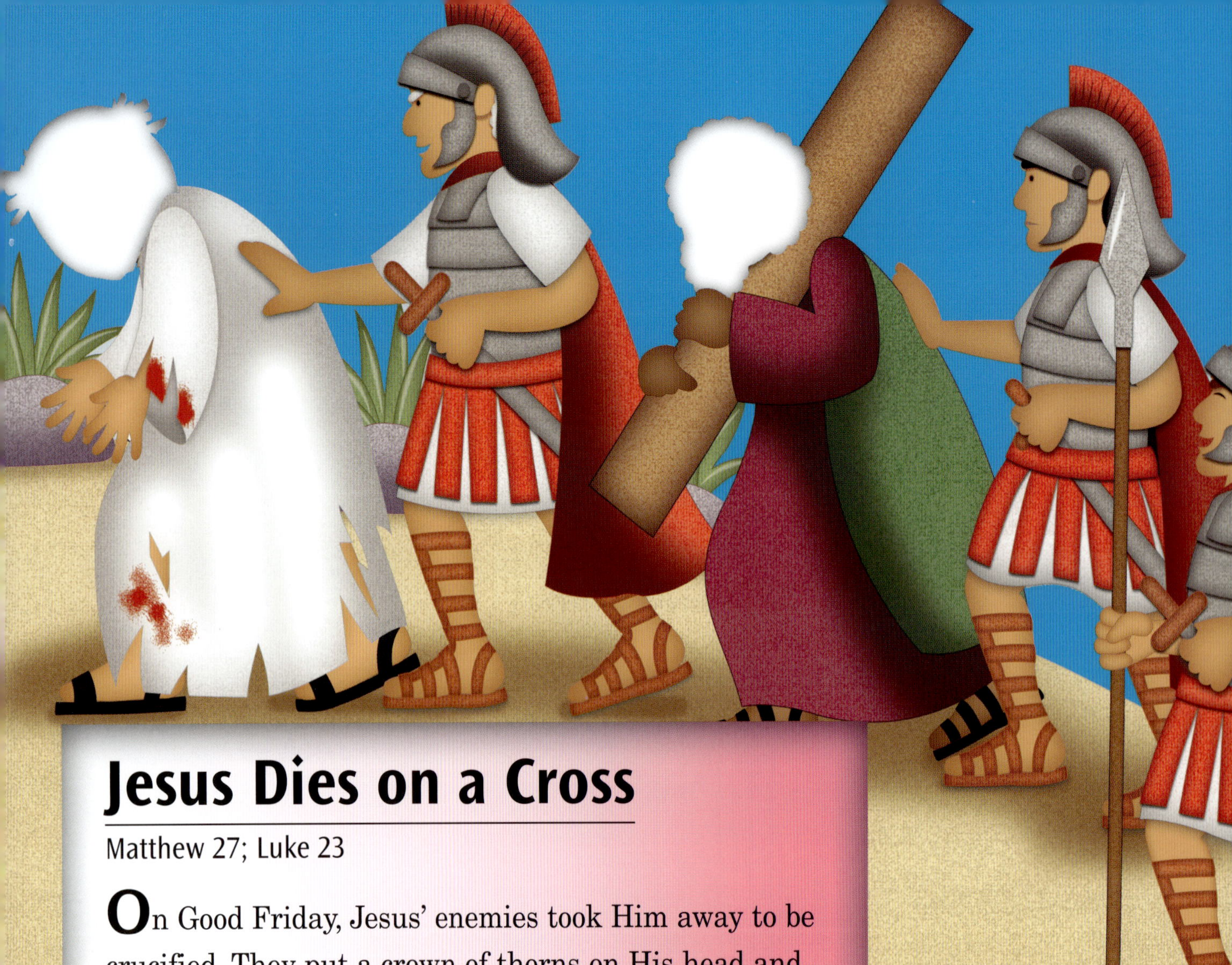

Jesus Dies on a Cross

Matthew 27; Luke 23

On Good Friday, Jesus' enemies took Him away to be crucified. They put a crown of thorns on His head and made Him carry the big heavy cross.

Jesus was so tired that He tripped and fell. Then the soldiers made a man called Simon carry the cross while they laughed and shouted.

The soldiers put Jesus on the cross. "Please forgive them," Jesus said to God. "They don't know what they're doing."

Then the sky grew dark, the temple curtain ripped in half, the ground shook, and Jesus died. He died for all the sins of all the people, even His enemies.

Later, some of Jesus' friends carried His body to a garden. Jesus was buried in a cool, dark cave. They rolled a huge, heavy stone across the entrance to the cave so no one could get in.

Add these grass stickers to the road.

Match the right head sticker to the right body.

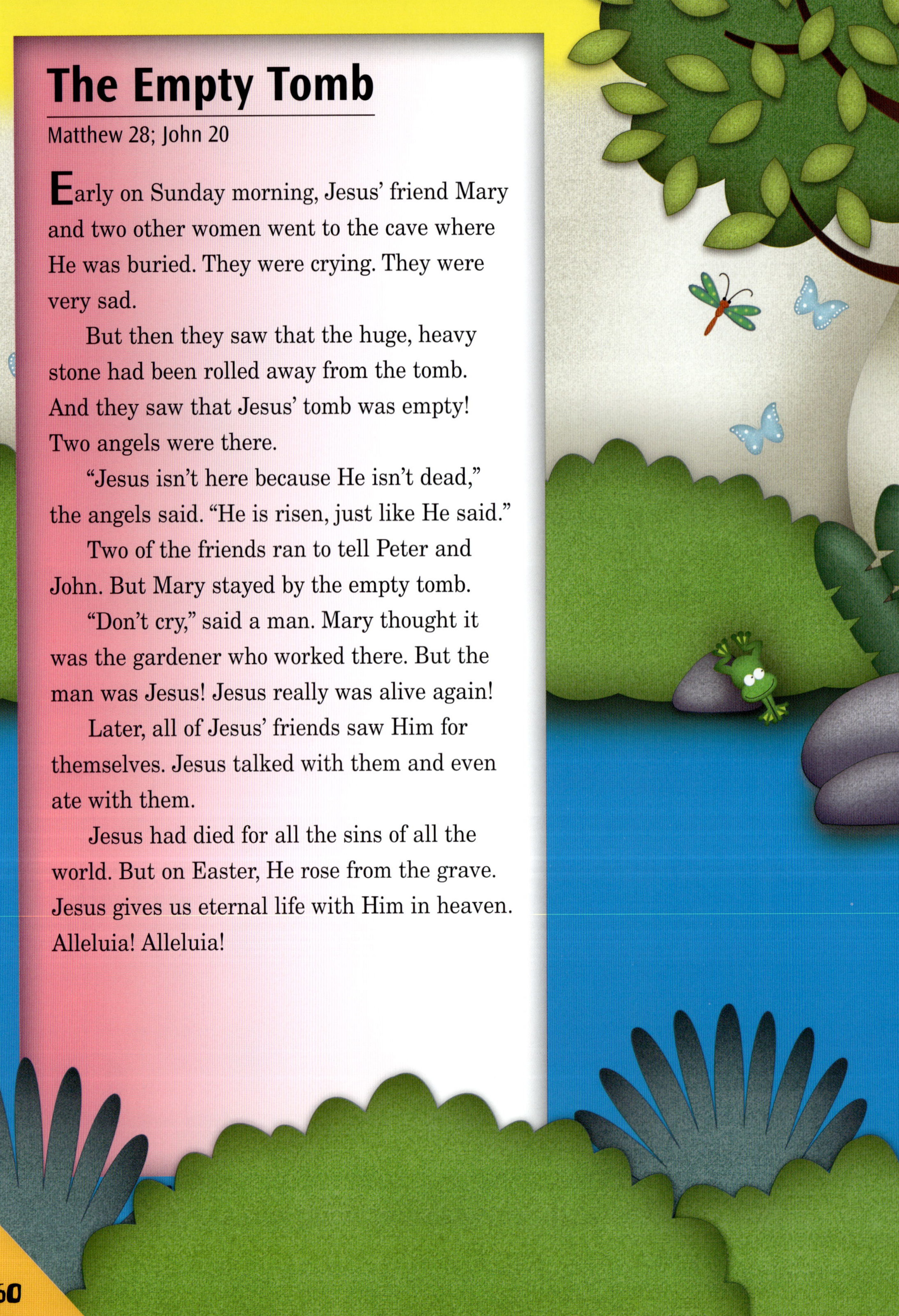

The Empty Tomb

Matthew 28; John 20

Early on Sunday morning, Jesus' friend Mary and two other women went to the cave where He was buried. They were crying. They were very sad.

But then they saw that the huge, heavy stone had been rolled away from the tomb. And they saw that Jesus' tomb was empty! Two angels were there.

"Jesus isn't here because He isn't dead," the angels said. "He is risen, just like He said."

Two of the friends ran to tell Peter and John. But Mary stayed by the empty tomb.

"Don't cry," said a man. Mary thought it was the gardener who worked there. But the man was Jesus! Jesus really was alive again!

Later, all of Jesus' friends saw Him for themselves. Jesus talked with them and even ate with them.

Jesus had died for all the sins of all the world. But on Easter, He rose from the grave. Jesus gives us eternal life with Him in heaven. Alleluia! Alleluia!

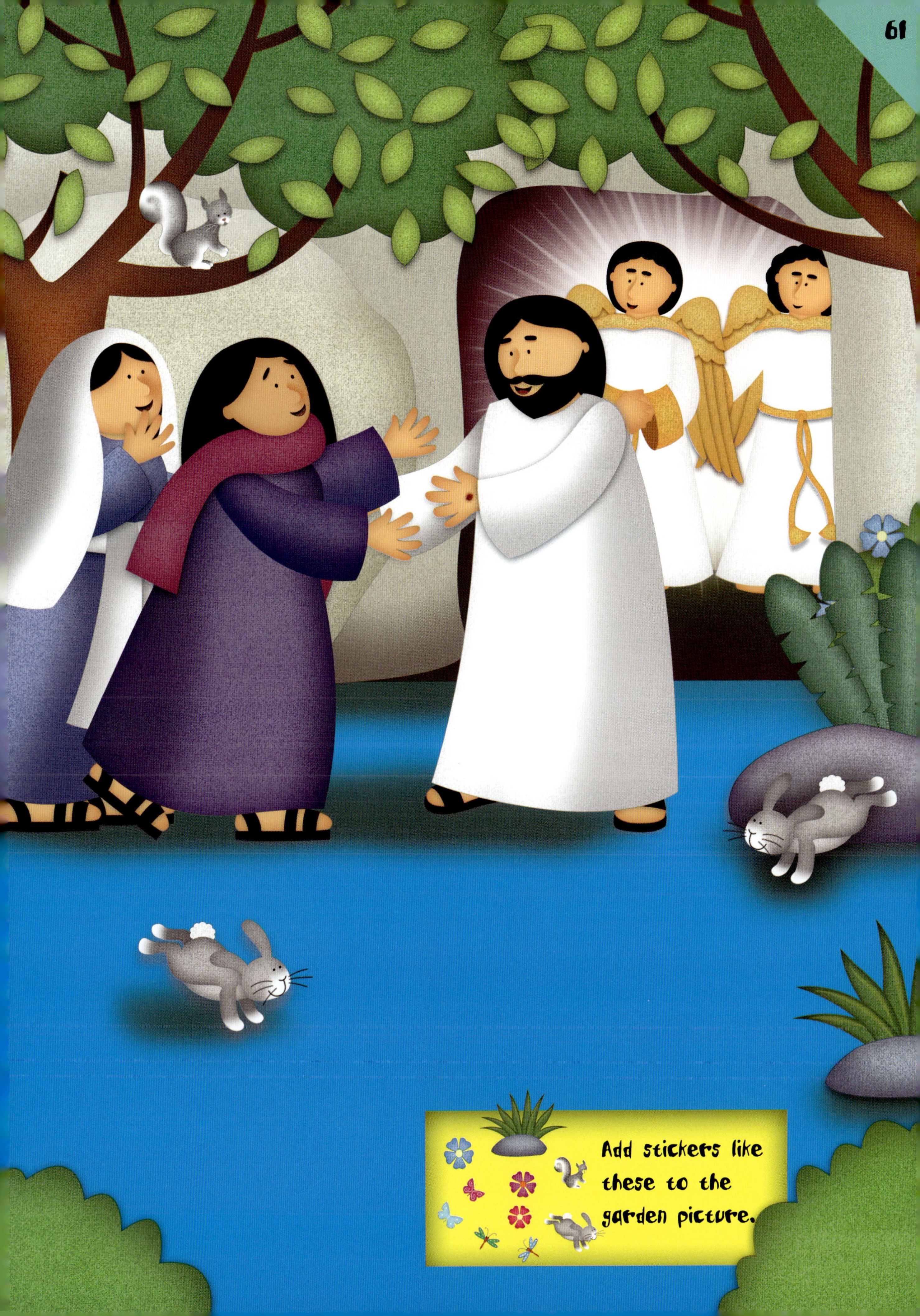
Add stickers like
these to the
garden picture.

Breakfast by the Lake

John 21:1–12; Matthew 28

Peter and his friends had fished all night, but they didn't catch any fish at all. Then, just as the sun was rising, they heard a man calling from the shore.

"Put your nets out on the other side of the boat!"

They did as the man said. Suddenly the net was full of fish—big and small and slippery and wet and wriggly.

"It's Jesus!" Peter and his friends shouted.

Jesus was on the shore, cooking fish.

The friends shared bread and fish with Jesus, and He told them that soon He would return to God in heaven.

"I will send you the Holy Spirit so you will have power to tell everyone about Me and about God," said Jesus. "You will never be alone. I will always be with you."

Find and use these three stickers.

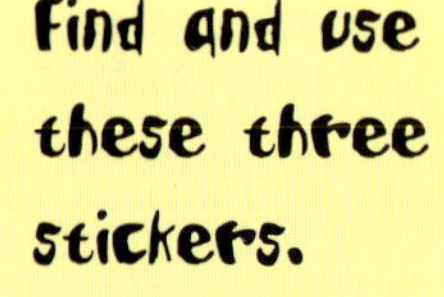

Put the bread stickers on the plates.

Add these leaves to the picture.

Put the
birds in
the sky.

This edition first published in 2017 by Concordia Publishing House
3558 S. Jefferson Avenue, St. Louis, MO 63118-3968
1-800-325-3040 • cph.org

Publishing Director: Annette Reynolds
Art Director: Gerald Rogers
Pre-Production Manager: Doug Hewitt
Manufactured in China/000920/417908

2-3
4-5
6-7
8-9
10-11

12-13
14-15
16-17
18-19
20-21

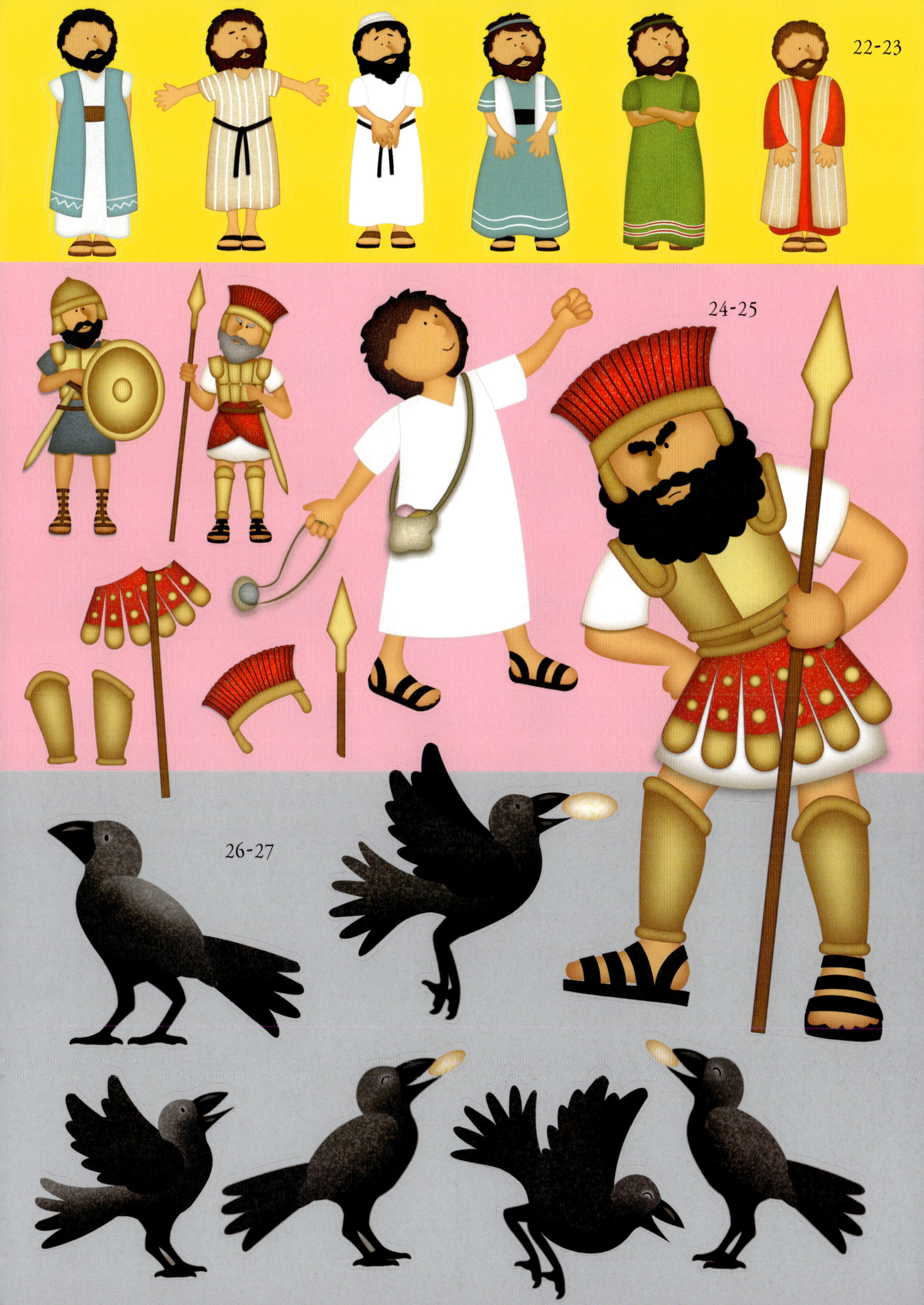

22-23
24-25
26-27

28-29

30-31

34-35
36-37
38-39
40-41

42-43
44-45
46-47
48-49
50-51

52-53
54-55
56-57
58-59

60-61

62.63

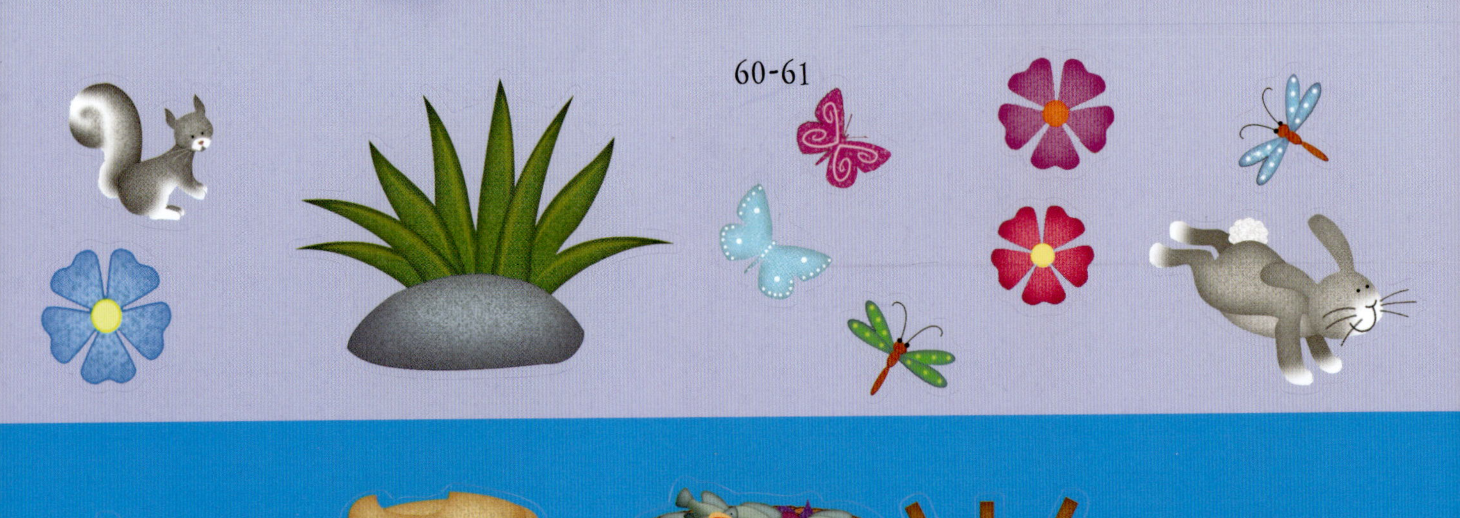

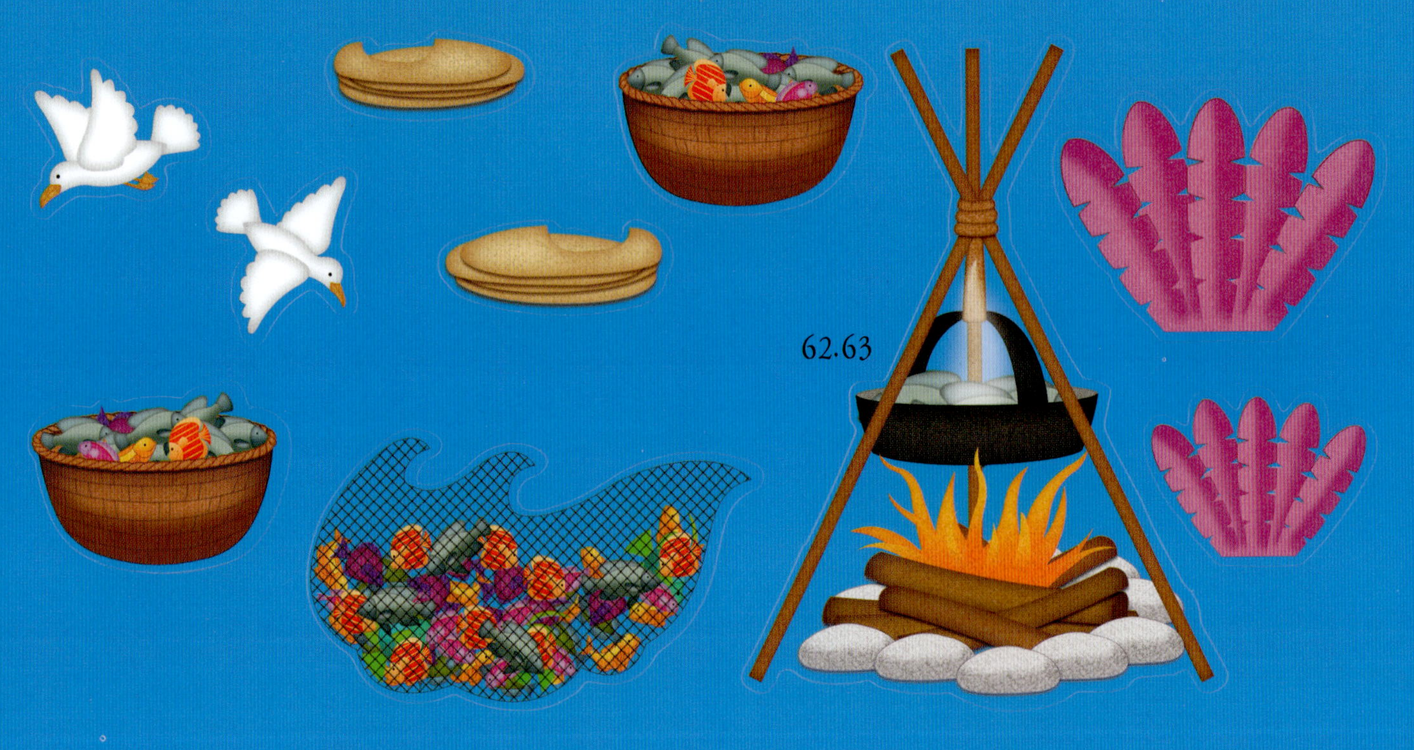

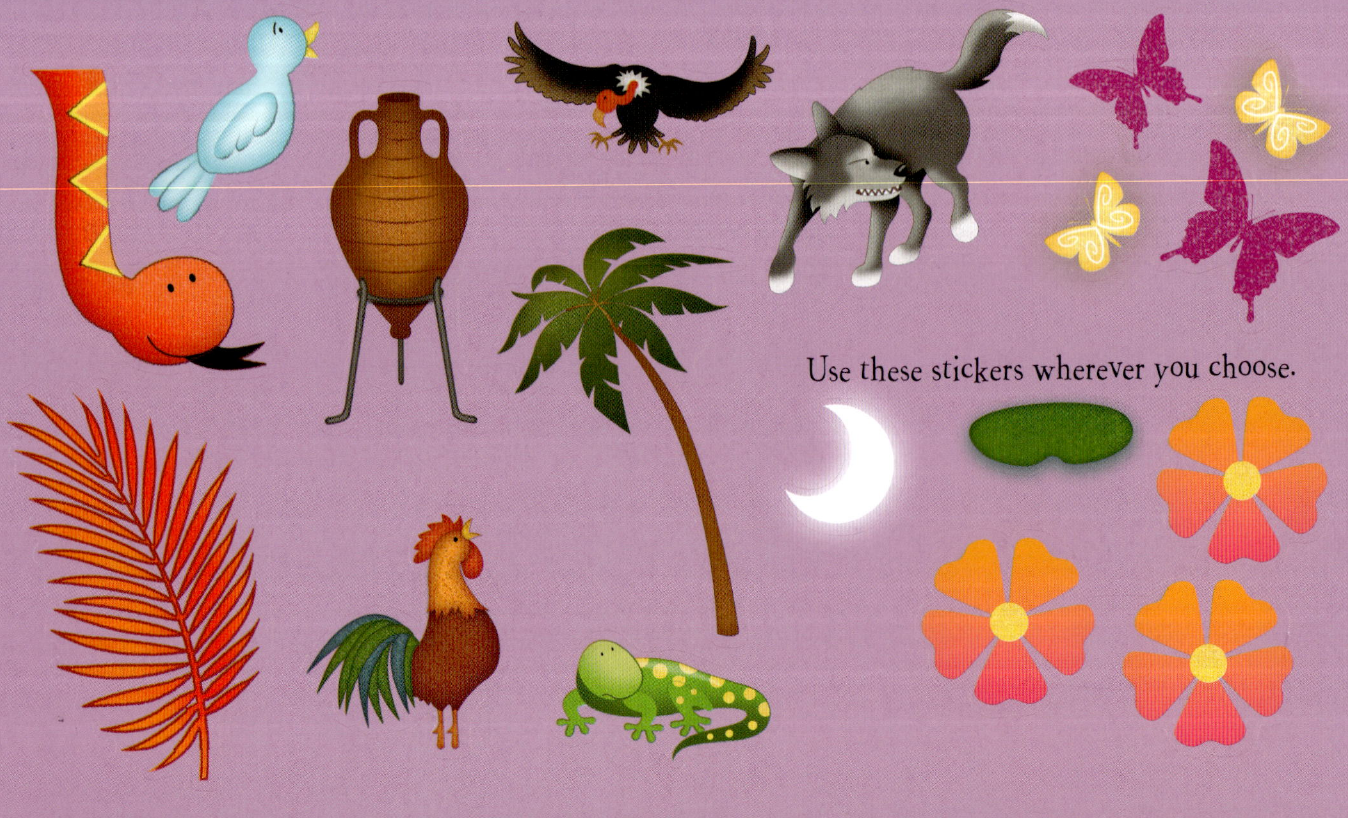

Use these stickers wherever you choose.